THE
LATIN
RIDDLE
BOOK

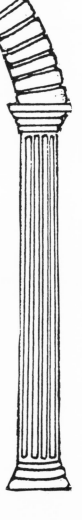

THE
LATIN
RIDDLE
BOOK

AENIGMATORUM
LIBER
LATINORUM

Illustrated by Joseph Farris

Compiled by Louis Phillips

Translated by Stan Shechter

Harmony Books/New York

Text copyright © 1988 by Louis Phillips and Stan Shechter
Illustrations copyright © 1988 by Joseph Farris

Published by Harmony Books, a division of Crown Publishers, Inc., 225 Park Avenue South, New York, New York 10003 and represented in Canada by the Canadian MANDA Group
HARMONY and colophon are trademarks of Crown Publishers, Inc.

Manufactured in the United States of America   .

Design by Ron McCutchan

Library of Congress Cataloging-in-Publication Data

Latin riddle book = Aenigmatorum liber Latinorum.

1. Riddles, Latin. I. Farris, Joseph. II. Phillips, Louis, III. Title: Aenigmatorum liber Latinorum.
PN6369.L38   1988   878'.002   88-11020

ISBN 0-517-56975-2
10 9 8 7 6 5 4 3 2 1
First Edition

for Ann and Carter Colwell (LJP)
for Carole, Linda, Alan, Jonathan, and Jez (SS)
for my wife, Cynthia C. Farris (JF)

I
CUR GALLINA PER VIAM TRANSIRE MALUIT?

UT IN ALTERA PARTE VIAE AMBULARET.

II

Cum ostenderit horologii virgula
spatium horarum tertium decimum
atque audieris totidem sonituum
claritates, quod tempus
significabitur?

Horologio novo utendi tempus.

III
Cur nasus in longitudinem unciarum duodenarum non crescit?

———

Si ad talem longitudinem pervenisset, pes esset.

IV

QUID ET COLORE ALBO ET PER ATRAMENTUM ATQUE OMNINO LEGENDUM?

ACTA PUBLICA.

V

IN NAVIBUS CUR CAESAR LAUDANDUS ERAT?

QUIA IDEM FUIT ROMANUS QUI PRAECLARISSIME REMIGABAT.

VI

QUID DICET MUS QUI LIBRAS PONDERIS
SESCENTAS ET MILLE EXSUPERET?

"HUC, HUC O FELES AD ME VENI, HUC,
HUC, O MI FELES."

VII

QUAE RES POSSIDET
DUODEVIGINTI CRURA
ET CAPTAT MUSCAS?

CATERVA EORUM
QUI PILA LUDUNT.

VIII

QUI CENTURIO GALEAM AMPLISSIMAM
GEREBAT?

IS QUI FUIT CAPITIS AMPLISSIMI.

IX

QUID FLAVESCIT EXTRA ALBESCITQUE
INTUS ET SONITU PROGREDITUR
CONCLAMANS "PUTTPUTTPUTT"?

———

MACHINA QUAE SIT NON SOLUM SPECIE ET
FIGURA ARIENAE SED ETIAM ADFIXA
LATERI NAVIS PROPELLENDI CAUSA.

X
QUID COLORE LIVIDUM NIGRUMQUE ATTAMEN CETERIS CANDIDIS?

===

ANIMAL ET QUOD ZEBRA VOCANT ET QUOD REFUTETUR ATQUE EX AEDIBUS EICIATUR PROBATIONE EQUORUM PRO LUDIS CIRCENSIBUS HABITA.

XI

Quomodo fieri potest ut infans moveatur e cunabulis?

Titillatio pedibus adhibenda.

XII

CUR ANAS QUAE AD MELIUS VIDENDUM
IMPOSUERAT VITREA ROTUNDA ROSTRO
SUO PER VIAM INCEDEBAT?

———

AD TABELLAS COTTIDIANAS EMENDAS
POPULI ROMANI.
(ME FUGIT.)
(NON EQUIDEM INTELLEGO. TEMPORA
NOVI EBORACI ACCIPIO CONSTANTER.)

XIII

CUR FERE PLURIMA SEPULCRA MOENIBUS
ALTIS CIRCUMSAEPTA SUNT?

———

QUIA TOT HOMINES SUNT QUI
ARBITRENTUR MORTEM IBI OPPETI POSSE.

XIV

SI CERVICIBUS TENUS TRES CAUSIDICI
SEPULTI IN HARENIS ERUNT, QUIDNAM
TENEBIS?

———

PARUM HARENARUM.

TIBI SALVE AIT POLUS GELIDUS

XV

QUID COLORE FULVO IN
SEPTENTRIONALIBUS VEL IN POLO
GLACIALI ERRAT ET CUI DUO
TUBERA SUNT?

NIHIL NISI CAMELUS QUI DE VIA DECEDIT.

XVI

QUIDNAM VIRET ET IN TOTO RUBESCIT ET
IN LITORE INVENITUR?

CUCUMIS E MURIA ATQUE OLLA, QUI SIT
USTUS A SOLE.

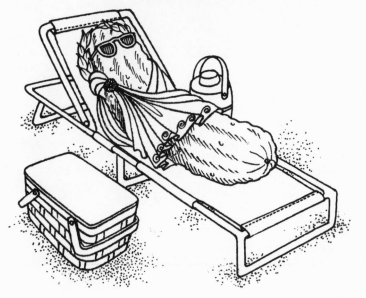

XVII
QUAE VERBA FACTA FUERANT IN
SUPREMIS A PICTURA IPSA?

"TUNC ME INCUSABANT ALICUIUS
CRIMINIS FICTI; NUNC ME SUSPENDERE
LIGNEIS E FORMIS VOLUNT."

XVIII

Quid melius est in opus pistorium inferre?

———

Tui dentes.

XIX

QUID OCTONA BRACCHIA HABET ET SUB AQUA INVENTUM EST?

DE QUADAM TONSTRINA QUATTUOR CANTATORES QUI IN PROFUNDA SUMMERSI SUNT.

XX

QUID INGENS, COLORE PLUMBEO, CUTEQUE
RUGOSA ATQUE IN SPELUNCA AETATEM
DEGIT INDIGENS?

RHINOCEROS CUI FIDES FUIT SAEPE
DENEGATA.

XXI
UTRUM CELERIUS? QUOD FIT CALIDUM AN QUOD FIT FRIGIDUM?

———

CALIDUM VERO, QUIA CUM FRIGORA
ERUNT NEMO EST QUI SUBITO NON
AFFLIGATUR STERNUMENTIS, TUSSIBUS,
CAPITIS DOLORE, DESTILLATIONIBUS
QUOQUE IN NARES.

XXII

MUSCA QUAE SUB NOCTEM DE CORPORE
FULGET SCINTILLIS AC QUAE CICINDELA
VOCATUR QUALEM SENSIT SE ESSE CUM
VOLAVERAT IN FLABELLUM QUOD ITERUM
ITERUMQUE MOVEBATUR AMBIENS EUNDEM
IN CIRCULUM VI QUASI E FULMINIBUS
GENERANDA?

———

MUSCA ILLA CANDIDISSIMAM ET
LAETISSIMAM PARUMPER SENSIT SE ESSE.

XXIII

QUOMODO CULICEM OPORTET MULGEAS?

———

AGE, PRIMUM MIRAE PARVITATIS SELLAM
ADIPISCARIS NECESSE EST.

XXIV

QUIS VICTUM CULTUMQUE POSSIT
NANCISCI DIURNIS SINE LABORIBUS?

———

XXXII　　IS QUI NOCTU VIGILIAS AGIT.

XXV
Quare apes murmure strepunt?

Quia verborum meminisse nequeunt.

XXVI
QUARE ISTE IMBECILLI
ANIMI RUSTICANUS
HOROLOGIUM
DE FENESTRA IECIT?

QUIA VOLUIT VIDERE QUOMODO
TEMPUS FUGERET.

XXXV

XXVII

QUID COLORIBUS PICTUM RUFO
CAERULEOQUE ET GLAUCO LUTEOQUE ET
FULVO NIGROQUE PURPUREO QUOQUE
INTUS, ETIAM CANDIDO EXTRINSECUS?

———

BINA FRUSTA PANIS INTRO ILLITA
TAMQUAM STILIS CEREIS QUI VARIOS IN
COLORES PIGMENTIS TRACTI SUNT.

XXVIII

Quid distinguitur colore et extrinsecus candido et intus flavo alboque, et de quo sonitus "cluc clic cluc" exprimitur?

═══════

Calamus ovi figura puncto atramenti scribens.

XXIX

REX MIDAS SI AUREO IN SOLIO SEDET,
QUIS IN SEDIBUS ARGENTOSIS?

PEREGRINATOR SOLITARIUS, CUI NOMEN
LONIO RANGERIO.

XXX

Quemadmodum fieri potest ut
Venetum caecum reddas?

———

Figendo digitos in oculis.

XXXI

QUODNAM VERBUM
RE VERE BREVIUS FIERI
POTEST SI DUAS
LITTERAS EI ADDES?

BREVE.

XXXII

QUID INTEREST INTER TIGRIM
LABORANTEM DENTIUM DOLORE AC
PARUM SERENUM DIEM?

———

ILLE GEMITU INGENTI INTONAT, HIC
IMBREM CUM TONITRIBUS NUNTIAT.

XXXIII

INTER DAMMAM QUAE A VENATORIBUS
FUGIT AC SAGAM PUSILLAM QUID
INTEREST?

DAMMA HAUDQUAQUAM NON VENANDA,
SAGA TAMEN VIX AMANDA.

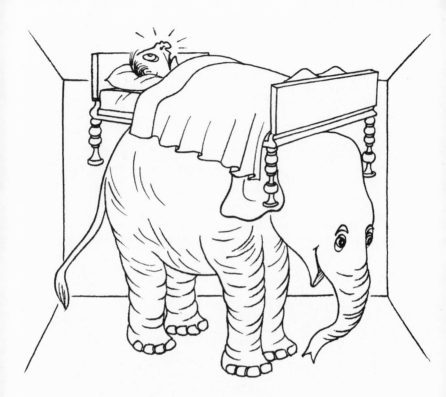

XXXIV

QUOMODO PERCIPI POTEST NUM SUB TUO
LECTULO LATEAT ELEPHAS?

═══════

NASUS ENIM TUUS SUB TIGNO INFIGETUR.

XXXV

QUID COLORE LUTEO CONSTAT ESSE PERICULOSISSIMUM?

SORBITIO EX OVIS FACTA SCATENSQUE PRISTIBUS.

XXXVI

QUOMODO SEPULTUS ERAT IS QUI SIGNIFICATIONES VERBORUM IN TRANSVERSUM OBSCURISSIMEQUE POSITORUM CONFICERE SOLEBAT?

═══════

IN TRANSVERSUM

I lator legis
II domus ruri
III vix ignavus
IV vis
V filia Ledae
VI comes fumo
VII colles septem

DESUPER

I gemma viridis
II aculeata
III aedes Iovis
IV casae
V equus Alexandri
VI amicus fidelis

VII

RESPONSA In Transversum I senator, II villa, III alacer, IV robur, V Helena, VI ignis, VII Roma **Desuper** I smaragdus, II vespa, III Capitolium, IV tuguria, V Bucephalus, VI canis

XLVI

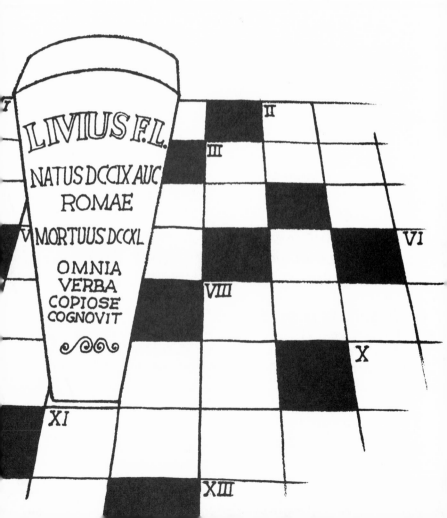

XXXVII

QUOD COGNOMEN DEBES ADDERE
CHAMAELEONTI QUI IN VIAM ET AUREAM
AC LATERICIAM IRREPSERIT?

LACERTA OZII.

XXXVIII

QUA DE CAUSA MAGISTRA IUXTA OCULOS
SUOS SEMPER PONEBIT VITREA OBSCURA ET
AD SIMILITUDINEM ORBICULI FORMATA
CUM TRADET PRAECEPTA STUDIOSIS
DISCENDI?

QUIA PUPILLAE SPLENDIDISSIMAE.

XXXIX

QUID FORAMINUM PLENUM AQUA
TENENTE?

SPONGIA.

XL

QUIDNAM VOCATUR EA MATERIES QUAE
INTER DIGITOS PEDUM HIPPOPOTAMI
FREQUENTER SITA EST?

═══════

CURSORES TARDIORES.

XLI

IN ALPHABETO QUOT LITTERAE SUNT?

=====

VIGINTI QUATTUOR; NAM E.T. DOMUM
REDIIT.

XLII

Postquam vir calvus pectinem natali
die suo nactus est, quid dixit?

"Non decet me huius doni participem
fieri."

XLIII
POLYPI COITU QUIDNAM
PARIT GALLINA?

PARIT AVEM QUAE TOT MULTIPLICES
CLUNES ET PECTORA HABEAT UT TOTI
FAMILIAE NON DIES SINE CARNE SIT.

LIII

XLIV

QUARE RUTILLISSIMA EX UMERIS CINGULA
GERUNTUR AB ILLIS QUI ADVERSUS
INCENDIA VIGILANTER INSTITUTI SUNT?

━━━━━

AD BRACAS SUSPENDENDAS.

XLV

ROMANO IMPERATORI
QUIBUS UTENDUM
EST UT FUNIS SECETUR?

CAESURAE
INSTRUMENTA.

XLVI
QUID DIXIT CINDERELLA FABRO QUI
CONFICIEBAT IMAGINES IAM LUCE
PARVOQUE IN SCRINIO QUODAM
STATIM FACTAS?

———

"ALIQUANDO," AIT, "AD ME PRINCEPS
MEUS ILLUSTRIS ADVENIET."

XLVII

QUID GIGNITUR EX HYAENA ET PSITTACO?

ANIMAL VIRIBUS RIDENDI IN IOCA SUA EXIMIUM.

THE
TRANSLATIONS

I   Why did the chicken cross the road?
To get to the other side.

II   When the clock strikes thirteen, what time is it?
Time to get a new clock.

III   Why is your nose not 12 inches long?
If it were 12 inches long, it would be a foot.

IV   What is black and white and red (read) all over?
A newspaper.

V   Why would Julius Caesar be good in a boat?
Because he was a noble row-man (Roman).

VI   What does a 1,200-pound mouse say?
"Here kitty, kitty, kitty."

VII   What has eighteen legs and catches flies?
A baseball team.

VIII   What centurion wore the largest helmet?
The one with the largest head.

IX   What is yellow on the outside, white on the inside, and goes "putt putt putt"?
An outboard banana.

X   What is black and white and black and blue?
A zebra thrown out of an audition for circus horses.

XI   How do you make a baby buggy?
Tickle its feet.

XII   Why did the duck wearing glasses cross the road?
To buy the Roman *Daily News*.
(I don't get it.)
(Neither do I. I get the *New York Times*.)

XIII   Why do they build high fences around cemeteries?
Because so many people are dying to get in.

XIV   What do you have when you have three lawyers buried up to their necks in sand?
Not enough sand.

XV   What is brown, has two humps, and is found in the North Pole?
A lost camel.

XVI   What is green and red
all over and found on
the beach?
A sunburned pickle.

XVII   What were the
painting's last words?
"First they frame me and
now they're going to hang me!"

XVIII What is the best thing to put into a pie?
Your teeth.

XIX   What has eight arms and is found underwater?
A drowned barbershop quartet.

XX   What is big, gray, wrinkled, and lives in a cave?
A rhinoceros with a poor credit rating.

XXI   Which is faster—hot or cold?
Hot is faster because anyone can catch cold.

XXII   How did the firefly feel when it met the electric
fan?
The firefly was de-lighted.

XXIII How do you milk a gnat?
Well, first you have to get a very low stool.

XXIV   Who can earn a living without ever having to
do a day's work?
A nightwatchman.

XXV   Why do bees hum?
Because they can't remember the words.

XXVI   Why did the silly Billy toss his alarm clock out the window?
Because he wanted to see time fly.

XXVII   What is red, blue, orange, brown, black, and purple on the inside, and white on the outside?
A crayon sandwich.

XXVIII   What is white on the outside, yellow and white on the inside, and goes "cluck, click, cluck"?
A ball-point egg.

XXIX   If King Midas sits on gold, who sits on silver?
The Lone Ranger.

XXX   How do you make a Venetian blind?
Stick a finger in his eye.

XXXI   What word actually becomes shorter if you add two letters to it?
Short.

XXXII   What's the difference between a tiger with a toothache and a stormy day?
One roars with pain while the other pours with rain.

XXXIII   What's the difference between a deer being chased and a midget witch?
One is a hunted stag, while the other is a stunted hag.

XXXIV How can you tell if an elephant is hiding under your bed?
Your nose is pressed against the ceiling.

XXXV What is yellow and very dangerous?
Shark-infested eggnog.

XXXVI How was the crossword-puzzle maker buried?
Six down, three across.

ANSWERS TO LATIN CROSSWORD PUZZLE

CLUES (across)		**ANSWERS** (across)
1	legislator	senator
2	country house	villa
3	opposite of lazy	eager
4	strength	strength
5	Leda's daughter	Helen
6	with smoke	fire
7	seven hills	Rome

CLUES (down)		**ANSWERS** (down)
1	green gem	emerald
2	has sting	wasp
3	temple of Jupiter	Capitol
4	huts	huts
5	Alexander's horse	Bucephalus
6	loyal friend	dog

XXXVII What do you call a chameleon on a yellow brick road?
The Lizard of Oz.

XXXVIII Why does the teacher insist upon wearing dark glasses to class?
Because her pupils are so bright.

XXXIX What is filled with holes, yet holds water?
A sponge.

XL What do you call the stuff between the toes of a hippopotamus?
Slow joggers.

XLI How many letters are there in the alphabet?
Twenty-four. E.T. went home.

XLII When the bald man received a comb for his birthday, what did he say?
"I'll never part with this."

XLIII What do you get when you cross a chicken with an octopus?
You get a bird that has enough drumsticks for the entire family.

XLIV Why do firemen wear red suspenders?
To keep their pants up.

XLV What does a Roman emperor use to cut a rope?
Scissors.

XLVI What did Cinderella say to the man developing her snapshots?
"Someday my 'prints' will come."

XLVII What do you get if you cross a hyena with a parrot?
An animal that laughs at its own jokes.